TAKE TWO: FILM STUDIES

TAKE TWO: FILM STUDIES

SUSAN TERRIS

OMNIDAWN PUBLISHING
OAKLAND, CALIFORNIA
2017

Cover photo by Bart Everson, from the Coca Cola filmstrip "Black Treasures" (1969)

Cover and interior set in Kabel LT STD and Joanna MT Std

Cover and interior design by Gillian Olivia Blythe Hamel

Offset printed in the United States
by Edwards Brothers Malloy, Ann Arbor, Michigan
On 55# Glatfelter B18 Antique
Acid Free Archival Quality Recycled Paper

Library of Congress Cataloging-in-Publication Data

Names: Terris, Susan, author. | Terris, Susan. Take two: Tears, Picasso &
    portrait of Dora Marr.
Title: Take two : film studies / Susan Terris.
Other titles: Take two: Tears, Picasso & portrait of Dora Marr.
Description: Oakland, California : Omnidawn Publishing, 2017.
Identifiers: LCCN 2017020883 | ISBN 9781632430472
    (paperback : alk. paper)
Classification: LCC PS3570.E6937 A6 2017 | DDC 811/.54--dc23
LC record available at https://lccn.loc.gov/2017020883

Published by Omnidawn Publishing, Oakland, California
www.omnidawn.com   (510) 237-5472   (800) 792-4957
10 9 8 7 6 5 4 3 2 1
ISBN: 978-1-63243-047-2

Table of Contents

Take Two: Tears

                                    I violate   self-satisfied
by the perfection of distortion   [abstract]   her three
breasts   round hole in a childless body   she is

butchered   crying   I love the blurred tracks from
eyes too close together   yes   a nose for an ear
a doormat   some women are   and the other Dora

thinks I left for Françoise   *women are machines*
for suffering   but the real Dora Maar   [alternate ending]
my muse   is here   the woman in tears   always

two-dimensionally mine   so each day   in one way
or another   I back her against a wall   gaze at those
bank-fish eyes   crazed body   [angle]   and hang her

then   boldly slash her with my name   *Picasso*

Take Two: Model Child

                    what is my real age   model
for painters   [blocking]   in Pittsburgh   New York   me
girl with a kissable bee-sting pout   then photographers

the stage   mother who sells me   looking for   [frame]
a rich man   to marry me or pay   Stanny pays
me   untouched   14 maybe   I love oysters   bon-bons

wind-up toys   my Red Riding Hood cape   and like
Alice   I'm girlish   famous   no books about me
yet   mother pretends to protect   looks away   I

pretend too   24th St. my Wonderland   but mother

off to Pittsburgh   leaves me   alone   with him

Stanford White   [swing]   champagne-drugged   I

wake in bed   he's naked   on my thigh   blood   no

more Wonderland   but scrambled passages   lies here

lies ahead   me and the White Rabbit   trapped   dark

blood   my name is Florence Evelyn   or Evelyn Nesbit

or Mrs. Harry Thaw   money or slut   [splice]   and mother

with pocket-money   is useless as the White Queen

Take Two: By The Book

married at 19   Italy   Switzerland   a wager

ghost story   [mix]   babies   dead babies   one son

her book   boats and water   her creature

a monster   wants love   her poet-husband wants

cronies   titillation   [racking]   new romance

he drowns   still the giant   at night   keeps

coming   hideous   yet consoling   sentient

will stroke her hair   [two shot]   and will not make

babies   days he hides   fiend so cold   Satan's

companion   slight ligaments   a fellow-devil
his face and body   at night   fallen yet bearable
love   unconditional   his head in her lap
or hers in his   in darkness they go   by ship   by rail

north and north   but headaches   [night-for-night]
tremors   something is happening   she grows
strange   tumor they say   but she knows more

after sunset   Mary Shelley's daemon gets bolder
scalpels   [final cut]   sutures   her single-minded lover
slices more of her delicate brain   to add to his

Take Two: Sidekicks

in the dark   plunge   he and I   three fathoms deep
amid moonless ruins   piteously   my friend moans
swallowed by a pit   [take]   I cry out in vain

to die would be a waste of good health

                                        and I feel
[day for night]   powerless   thinking toads   snakes
our bones gnawed white   my friend is old and rather

weak   what to do   self-comfort by approach from
the rear   not a sanctioned Catholic act   nor would it be
if I dispatch him   and with my sword   feast on

tough flesh   so how much does honor pay per hour
look   to my laments   he listens   does not say
a stupid word   if we survive   I'll crown him

poet laureate   to him   I feed my last pocketful
of crumbs   [aerial shot]   with bread all sorrows lessen
others call him Dapple   to me he is donkey or ass

sigh   ass   my addled knight   Quixote   not trapped
in a smooth-walled pit   is somewhere sliding off
Rocinante   [pull back]   while   alas   I feel my belly

shrink   as I ponder faith   loyalty   self-preservation
I   Sancho Panza   fat pudding stuffed with proverbs

Take Two: Alley-Time

this writer's not Kafka   his vermin soul   fate
types lowercase   whotthehell   his good friend
she   of amber eyes and loose hair [oscar bait]

she   who feels transmogrified   from a life as
cleopatra [flash forward]   lovely this love   but
not hot   obstacles abound   size and fuzz

he's a kind of minor poet   brings her lightness
   both share wit and tell   yet live for the dark
whotthehell   [smash cut]   both prowl the night

alley-time   she likes vermin   and he smarts   he does
but size matters   and he's so small [pace]   archie
yearns   mehitabel burns   well then   eat me   he sez

Take Two: Novel Pick Up

Because Beaudelaire calls me   stupid slut   I try to prove
him right   you see   I'm on semi-permanent leave
from fiction   and marriage   my composer applauds

but he's grey   so by night   my sport   catch-and-release
pants and waistcoat   [cinéma vérité]   with cravat   cubebs
I prowl Montmartre's nameless cafés   [mise-en-scène]

drink sour wine   chum for willing flesh   ah   look there
belle or beau in woman's frock   rouged lips   fringed
eyes cut in my direction   [match cut]   I'll take her/him

while Chopin   who calls me muse   writes a last mazurka
I rise   meet the mark's eyes   blow him/her a smoky halo of
a kiss   angle away   behind me soft steps   then   a voice

androgynous   asks   *pardon but are you*   *George Sand*

Take Two: Fabular Lies

an uncle/king   nephew/son   Irish princess
the king's bride   nephew her escort   [skypan]   but
a forest   fox and ferns   love potion for two

no dream yet of midsummer's night   no ass head
but bride de-brided   yet wed to the king
an infernal triangle   from the king   golden plums

from her lover   his plums   sin or compulsion
the tale is complex as m'lady's braided crown
[prelap]   then poisoned lance strikes nephew/son

harp or rescue   from afar   Yseult   the tell

white sails or black   lies   Tristan's mouth foams

white   [false ending]   dies   Yseult dies

King Mark shreds his garments   but think time

travel   dense braid of fabular deceit   lovers undead

flee   forest retreat   honeysuckle and hazel

intertwine   [remake]   endure   until spring forward

three centuries   when Mark morphs to Arthur

Tristan to Lancelot   both mad for sexy Y/Queen G

Take Two: Born in Fire

named after a gypsy queen   [jump cut] my life
if ever mine played out in headlines   he stole
me   my story   ballet fever they said

demon-flame   I the singed swan   yet he
no Siegfried   [arc shot]   what we did was
never real   only seared days to reassemble

on paper   booze the besting mistress   no that's
a damned lie   she drinks from your orifices
picks your pockets   and now all the flappers

are dead   even me   the rosin box   missing

the barre too high   our passports stamped

for the wrong destination   [diffusion]   my fires

hot   then hotter   Scott has asbestos hands

        asbestos soul   flocks

of jazz-age butterflies have forgotten to flap

[looping]   he ignites   until he doesn't   can't

Zelda   un-Zelda-ed   instead of Fitz

just fizz   both of us   rendered sparkless

Take Two: It's All Greek

I speak   *Savura*   not with whispers like yours
[sotto voce]   but my own loud   if faultering
bel canto   to say   he was never yours

a piece of paper   money promised   betrayal
comes in disguise   he said you   *Scylla*   little
coathanger of Cassini-gowns   were only vanilla

did you not know   how often we two were
in Monte Carlo or asea near Scorpios   to screw
[lap dissolve]   spoon up caviar   and screw

so delicious   your jewels were meaningless
only I knew how to polish his   and when he knew
death was near   he took to the hospital

the deep-red blanket   wrapped himself in it
my last gift   bloody-strong   our love   now he's
gone   and I the grieving widow   [out-take]

yes   I am Callas   to you   Jacqueline
I send raspberries and catcalls

Take Two: Familiar Tense

no diaries   no other letters   only this
when Mary's Belgian griffon died   the painter
wrote   asking friends   to find her a new dog

[clip]   she was thirty-three   autumn in Paris
and send it to her by parcel post   she desires
a young dog   a very young one that will love her

two artists together   again and again   he paints her

[dailies]   yet restraint   she glazes his oils
he adds highlights to hers   careful not to nudge
with his elbow   loathe to let flesh spoil luster

the new pup in her arms   she leans forward
[pull back]   a shadow union   he feels the heat
of her breath   *like the autumn we met*   *let's*

risk   she murmurs   *don't*   he cautions
I'm just an old man who likes horses as you like dogs
        Mary Cassatt strokes the dog's muzzle

its silken warmth   [mask]   *when we met*   she
says   *then*   *I began to live*   Degas leans back
in the bentwood chair   closes his eyes   *tais toi*

he says   *be still*

Take Two: Special Relativity

Speed of light in a vacuum   first before marriage
specific gravity   our giveaway girlchild
two scientists   scientists measure passion too

his counted   not mine   always alpha then beta
[aperture]   I agreed   we wed   velocity   two boys
those fast moving bodies   but then curved space

mistress-cousin   it's all relative   his drawn contract

neutered   made me   de-facto   no continuity
neither speech nor sex permitted   [fisheye lens]
I took the boys   left   yet that's not what you

want   [godspot effect]   you ask for   the red spread
Elsa   plates hurled   tears   the tearing of hair
we physicists seek free-falling states   time

dilation   those elementary particles   knowledge
is never filmic   what you need is
the why of Nobel cash   [reel]   what divorce

terms promised for a prize   not-yet-won
why I never said I helped   [negative cut]   was it
all Einstein   that constant speed   or Mileva too

me   with money
bribed again   [focus then fade]   for silence

Take Two: His Suicides

E: such a vain and stupid girl his poppet/puppet
he humors her   soirées   glitz   doctor school
a waste when he has me   and my photographs
[rushes]   his dreams   and worlds to conquer

G: ah yes   Uncle Alf   people suspect   does he
do we   a dewy girl   I live with him   [key grip]
he loves   [gaffer]   we do play   and play house

E: she's chubby   doesn't know I told A.H. about
the chauffeur   then he yanked her   kept his pet
locked up   but   backfire   [fade]   no time left

G: model despises me   *blöde Kuh*   longs
to know   do I kneel and unzip   does he tell
me to hop up on my knees   be his doggie

G: hate-love-hate   Frau Eva   *dumme Schlampe*

E: I tease and taunt   my first death tries   not
serious   just for emphasis   [leitmotif]   I know
power   as he does   and he has work to do

G: for me   no key   no life   but I'll triumph
Geli   his gun   my hand   to my chest
Angel-a   his true love lost

E: Wulf is mine now   his home   *mein Campf*
mein Fuhrer   might   his Eva   we win
then lose   but we marry   will die together
Geli erased   and for me   [arc light]   fame   glory

Take Two: Dashboard Scene

passenger seat   arrows   boots on the dashboard
cowboy toes and frayed heels   but women's boots
leather-laced   and it's a truck   on the left

steering wheel on the left too   long mid-western
road forks ahead   [pan]   circles   maybe a gyre
a dark steel quonset hut   black-and-white magpies

she rides shotgun   feet on the dashboard
asks   *did my mother do this at my age   did yours*
arrows are invisible   yet there   they prick her flesh

radio gone   truck speeds by   if she is smoking
we can't see or smell it   but we know   in her lap
[dolly shot]   she cradles the guns

        what is down the dotted line of the road
is this Bonnie   is that Clyde driving the wrong
side   yes   [master shot]   they don't know   now

even closer   magpies   they croon
how someone *lies over the ocean*   croon 'til they see
a road block ahead   *stop*   she cries   *stop now*

Take Two: The Bloodied Bed

he is slain   and we are in the burgundy chamber
half-hidden by arras   knife   much blood   little
struggle   more a death-dance   then nothing

he seems to breathe   yet not   men come   roll
the body in brocade swags   bear it away   now
we are alone   [close-up]   a table   a candle   a key

a feather too   we place the key   the feather   in
our robe's pocket   try out   the bloodied bed
then rising   lift the candle   creep into the next

room   there we watch   as golden wax scalds
our hand   drips onto stone   and men tend
the corpse   [splice]   when his body's oiled   we

no I   Lady Macbeth   bend to kiss his lips   but he
eases from the pallet   Duncan becomes an arching
shadow   palms the feather   the key   snuffs

the candle   we are chilled   here tonight   Duncan
came   and purposed to leave   and he leaves us
now   here   bloodied   and darkly alone   [cut]

Take Two: Immortal

call us the lost ones   the slain   [flip]   young bones
and blood   cry out   beneath this marble tomb
don't name our mother   unless you pause

passerby   I am a mute rock but these inscriptions

name our father   mother murdered for the fleece
then his new wife-to-be   yet not us   whom Hera
swore immortal   *stop*   our mother howled

tried to shield us   but no knife
fierce   [flashback]   men of Corinth stoned us

battered   bloodied   left   death-in-life
Medea   born of Circe   mother-sorceress
could not conjure us back   no mandrake

must speak   so you know who hides within me

or balm   while Jason   false father   fled
we are   Mermerus and Pheres   [wipe]   abandoned
by the Corinth Odeum   this   our immortality

no chariot race skyward   and over Styx   no ferry

Take Two: She-Fiend

old tale   a mother   son dead   bereft   greedy for
man-blood   she-fiend   not misshapen wolf-monster
[ellipsis]   but woman   nails and sword

to kill her   Hero of Heorot   must defy fen-spirits

moor-walkers   [flux]   past earthlight into
hell-cursed water   the Geat breeches death
in murked-mere   with writhing water-worms

as dark mad-brute woman   claws   drags with
nail-teeth   to sea-chill rockchamber   and tops
him   orgy   struggle   he-she   in cave-fire light

she-demon   death-grind   she on his chest
fire-eyes   Beowulf manned and unmanned
penetration   revenge   [fog level]   the little death

another come   his weapon weak   mantis-like she
wants his head   but he hefts her sword
beheads   her dead son Grendel too   mere-blood

Grendel's gore-head speared then   and lofted

consummation   [long take]   waters roil-red
Beowulf   defiled but still alive

Take Two: Kill Off

always the other other
[ambient light]   her mentors   lovers   sculpted
beauty in a bonnet   the famous

molded her   [climax/anticlimax]   lyrical talent
world in clay   lost wax and bronze   hands
hers on him   him in hers   not chaste

but chased   erotic studio chaos   bronze waltz
slicked with fresh clay   in her kiln
still always that other woman   the wilted rose

he won't drop   Camille rages   melts his waxes

[kill off]   hammers his clay   spills slurry   *bébé*

gone   from her he stole   unhinged   she set

studios on fire   [new storyboard]   enter her brother

straightjacket   barred cell   never Debussy

no sea-swells   traitors   no key   for Rodin

[framing]   *Kiss*   *Burghers of Calais*

his old Rose   for Mad'moiselle Claudel   30 years

locked in   [deep focus]   communal grave

Take Two: 1887 Fame

she is   done   done   a stick-in-the-mud flanked

by me   already 26   no flair   midget-woman

while I'm   big and comely   with bouncy bosoms

swell-swivel hips   whereas   that apple-pan-dowdy

is shaped like her gun   and I   just 15   [foil]

get the misters   the prizes   fame   see my ruffle-busting

duds   my pretty feet   I do tricks too   in the ring

on a mattress   and I *am* a crack shot   [eyeline match]

anything she can   I do hotter   longer   better

she's a ha-ha-hasbeen   at Beaver Bill's Wild West thing

gone today   goner tomorrow   no one will recall

Annie Oakley   it's *me* that the whole effin' world

[coda]   will fall for   Miss Lillian Smith   *me*

Take Two: Hung

enter the husband   swazzle   enter the wife
they embrace   kiss   her hat slips over one eye
dummy   she says   [blow-up]   he hits her

on the head   she grabs the club   clobbers him   [still]
now watch the baby   she says   tossing the child
he drops it   blockhead   wife hits him again

husband says   what a brave fellow I am   but behind
creeps an alligator who says   I'll eat you   wife says
no   please eat me   [action]   Punch clubs her

enter the hangman   says   I will string you up   sir
you dropped the baby   hit your wife   oh yes
yells Judy   then   sweet hangman   come and rope me

Take Two: Star-Takers

for each sin   in time   [reverse angle]   asks of us
asks the we   of us   breasts   brief   heedless
night steps   on stone floors   her chamber   mine

yes   her uncle's house   Paris   servants mum
she   girl-woman   *nominatissima*: intellect
renowned   and I   he   philosopher-scholar

my tutor in theory   in medicine   in company
subtle   yet   a house can be chill
so in the dark   down pillow lolls   comforters

his hands beneath my shift   bedcreaks   cries
            then   I fell pregnant with his child
our Astrolabe star-taker   and marriage   [backlit]

too late for us   for my Héloïse a nunnery
[soft focus]   for my Abélard the knife   the we
of us severed   like his   no   like my manhood

our letters cold   mind ticks   shadows   the we
now   [voice-over]   only I and I

Take Two: Crosscut

tricked out in gay ruffles   feathers   mesh hose
we choose to be   girly-bait   saunter
streets alone   yet together   the London fog

slimes us   wet mackerel smell   perfume
          clicks of our worn boots on cobbles
one pair scarlet   one toad green   as he

[tilt shot]   strolls our shite-pocked lanes   cane
leather apron slung as a cape   his tall top hat
satined by dank air   gestures   we nod

link arms   lead him to a room   a bed   he laughs

high sharp sounds   but under our cloaks
        knuckledusters   notched blades   cudgels
he flashes his knife   but Whitechapel rules   we

are two   faster   our blades   blood
thrust   [pull back]   mutilate   we slash
his coat vest and shirt   no more sister deaths

but on his hairless chest   chemise   bound breasts
no Jack here   a Jill   [fade to black]

sever   cut   cleave   dump in the Thames
done   the Ripper is done   [catharsis]
she is   forever   stopped

Take Two: Whatever Self

last night   we had a dream   [fade]   the nerve of pleasure
easily numbs   a disconnected rhapsody
but we read books and write them   have a husband

a woman lover   in the garden   already
snow drops   now   copying our recipe for cottage loaf
now re-reading Byron's Don Juan   and gorging on

Jane Austen   Rebecca West says men are snobs   but
though we are   jam and butter   Leonard is not   we

shy in the shadows today   the little owl
is calling   keeps calling   to silence him
we permit Clive to visit   then Lady Colefax

[dissolve]   when Conrad died   we wrote something   what
Clarissa is important   why   here is a nervous breakdown
in miniature   yesterday we had *daube de boeuf*   then

last night   the dream   the waves   waves   we are
re-editing the death chapter   though we don't get
out of bed   but shadows thin   we have tea   look at

antiques   then   ants in our brain   painted flies
in glass cages   for there we were   in last night's dream
with rocks   [follow-shot]   walking into the Ouse

it's dark now   darker   one of the Virginias must stir
make us   a simple supper of haddock and sausage

Take Two: Drowning

one floor is hay   one salt   one sand   stairs
a warehouse   many stairs   dark and we are
running   [zoom]   a boardroom table   men

with rags on their feet   slide and polish it   they
wrestle   then fight   there's a knife   one runs
plush drapes part   we follow   he's gone

stairs and more stairs   a man dressed as Punch
a fish tank   a Judy-woman pushes his peaked
head deep   water splashes   his face balloons

then   a gasp   he jerks up   runs   we follow
ballroom of sand   [reaction shot]   sequined harlots
strip him naked   other men come   an orgy

a new knife flashes   we are holding hands

now   as two bearded men fight   over and

in and out of a '54 Chevvy   Wozzeck is here

Marie watches from a slatted porch swing

    but there's an audition   for ingenues   and

when they try to paint our faces   we flee

running   again   someone falls   yet not us

[cutaway]   there's a hill of salt   and a pool of dank

water   hundreds of bird-masked figures

watch   there's another sharp knife   blood

a struggle   screaming   a drowning   then

lights lit   masks off   champagne   [it's a wrap]

Film Terms List

abstract
action
aerial shot
alternate ending
ambient light
angle
aperture
arc light
arc shot
backlit
blocking
blow-up
catharsis
cinéma vérité
climax/anticlimax
clip
close-up
coda
cutaway
cut
dailies
day-for-night
deep focus

diffusion
dissolve
dolly shot
ellipsis
eyeline match
fade
final cut
flip
fade to black
false ending
finale
fisheye lens
flashback
flash forward
flux
focus then fade
fog level
foil
follow shot
frame
framing
gaffer
godspot effect

it's a wrap
jump cut
key grip
kill off
lap dissolve
leitmotif
long take
looping
mask
master shot
match cut
mise-en-scène
mix
new storyboard
night-for-night
Oscar bait
out-take
pace
pan
prelap
pull back
racking
reaction shot

reel
remake
reverse angle
rushes
shock cut
skypan
smash cut
soft focus
sotto voce
splice
still
swing
swish pan
take
tilt shot
two shot
voice-over
wipe
zoom

Notes

This book is a series of filmic scenes about pairs (not always humans) heading toward trouble, disaster, or death. A quick reference, as you read, is available in the **Table of Contents**. Below you will find descriptions of the cast for each scene:

Take Two: Tears

The pair in this opening sequence are artist Pablo Picasso and a portrait of Dora Maar. A photographer, she was Picasso's muse for a decade—starting in the late 1930s. . . until she wasn't.

Take Two: Model Child

Here, the duo here are Evelyn Nesbit at 14 and her mother. Evelyn was a child when her mother began to shop her around as a model, chorus girl, and potential wife—yes, the one in the middle of the triangle when her husband Harry Kendall Thaw murdered her lover, architect Stanford White.

Take Two: By the Book

Not Mary Shelley and her poet husband, Percy, but Mary and the Monster she created in her novel *Frankenstein* are featured here. Sometimes love, even dangerous love, is where you find it.

Take Two: Sidekicks

In this take, Sancho Panza, from the novel *Don Quixote* (1605-15), and his donkey Dapple are the pair who have tumbled into a deep crater.

Take Two: Alley Time

archy the cockroach and mehitabel the cat are from a series by Don Marquis begun in 1916. archy, "the poet," typed lowercase, because he couldn't depress the capital key.

Take Two: Novel Pick-Up

This is a noir view of the 19th century French novelist Amatine-Lucile-Aurore Dupin, who wrote under the name of George Sand. A woman with many lovers, she prowled Montmartre at night, dressed in men's clothing, looking for excitement.

Take Two: Fabular Lies

Yseult was a 12th century Irish princess who fell in love with Tristan on her way to marry his uncle, King Mark. At the end of the many versions of the Celtic legend, both are dead. Maybe.

Take Two: Born in Fire

Is it necessary, after all, to say how Scott Fitzgerald and his wife Zelda destroyed one another? Blame it on Scott? Say alcohol? Say Zelda was mad? You decide.

Take Two: It's All Greek

Opera singer Maria Callas and Jacqueline Kennedy were both attached to Aristotle Onassis—one as lover and one as wife. This is Maria's message to Jackie after Onassis dies.

Take Two: Familiar Tense

American painter Mary Cassatt and French painter Edgar Degas were great friends with much restraint. And, yes, he did write a letter about finding a dog for her.

Take Two: Special Relativity

Albert Einstein and his first wife Mileva were both physicists. The trouble here is the never-explained question of whether she helped to develop his Theory of Relativity. Did she?

Take Two: His Suicides

Adolph Hitler's half-niece Geli Raubal and his woman friend Eva Braun were fierce competitors. This piece uses both of their voices, as they trash one another.

Take Two: Dashboard Scene

Yes, this is about the infamous robbers and killers Bonnie Parker and Clyde Barrow on the road shortly before they were ambushed, the moment of their not knowing yet knowing. . . .

Take Two: The Bloodied Bed

Here we have Lady Macbeth, referring to herself in plural tense, as she witnesses the murder of King Duncan and its aftermath. Note: this is before she starts to wash blood from her hands.

Take Two: Immortal

After their deaths, Mermerus and Pheres, Medea's sons, offer an alternate version of the hands at which they died. Believe them or not: it's all a myth.

Take Two: She-Fiend

In a cave, Beowulf, hero of a long poem in Old English (circa 1000) and the mother of the monster Grendel struggle erotically as she tries to avenge the murder of her son. Yes, there will be blood.

Take Two: Kill Off

Camille Claudel was a young woman sculptor (when there were almost none) and lover of sculptor Auguste Rodin. The trouble and her calamitous collapse came when he would not abandon Rose Beuret, who'd been his lover for 20 years.

Take Two: Fame

Annie Oakley was 26 when Bill Hickok hired a lusty 15 year old sharpshooter named Lillian Smith for his Wild West Show. It's Lillian who describes herself and her rival here.

Take Two: Hung

This pair: puppets -- Punch and Judy of *Commedia del Arte* fame, fighting as always. "Hit me? I'll hit you back!" A few other traditional puppets crash the scene.

Take Two: Star-Takers

Classic lovers: Héloïse and Abélard: what could go wrong? Only everything. A brilliant nun and a compelling philosopher thrown together in a cold house somewhere around 1132 when they were young seekers. Voice-over here is spoken by both.

Take Two: Crosscut

The duo here are a pair of prostitutes, circa 1889, who come upon Jack the Ripper on a murky London night. The murder of the Ripper, as told here, reveals a long-held secret. Shhhh!

Take Two: Whatever Self

And in this scene, Virginia Woolf struggles with Virginia Woolf a short time before the walk into the River Ouse. Yes, two distinct personalities, two voices in turmoil.

Take Two: Drowning

In the last sequence [It's a wrap]: Franz Woyzech and Marie from an unfinished 1836 play by Georg Buchner: two lovers, soldiers, a murder, and drownings. Alban Berg's 1922 opera *Wozzeck* is the best known finished version.

Acknowledgments

Colorado Review, "Take Two: Sidekicks / Sancho Panza & his Donkey Dapple"

Blue Fifth Review, "Take Two: Tears / Piccaso & Portrait of Dora Maar," "Take Two: Alley Time / archy & mehitabel," "Take Two: Immortal / Medea's Sons - Memeris & Pheres," "Take Two: Star-Takers / Abélard & Héloïse"

Diode, "Take Two: Kill Off / Auguste Rodin & Camille Claudel"

Marsh Hawk Review, "Take Two: Familiar Tense / Mary Cassatt & Edgar Degas," "Take Two: Hung / Punch & Judy," "Take Two: It's All Greek / Maria Callas & Jacqueline Kennedy"

Room (formerly *A Room of One's Own*), a much earlier version of "Take Two: Familiar Tense" titled "In a Familiar Tense"

Forgotten Women Anthology, Grayson Books, "Take Two: Fame / Annie Oakley & Lillian Smith"

An expanded version of "Take Two: Whatever Self / Virginia Woolf & Virginia Woolf" was presented as a micro play as part of Avant GardARAMA at the Cutting Ball Theater in San Francisco, October 2016.

Susan Terris' most recent books are *Memos* (Omnidawn Publishing) and *Ghost of Yesterday: New & Selected Poems* (Marsh Hawk Press). She is the author of 6 books of poetry, 16 chapbooks, 3 artist's books, and one play. Journal publications include *The Southern Review*, *Colorado Review*, *Georgia Review*, and *Ploughshares*. A poem of hers from FIELD appeared in *Pushcart Prize XXXI*. A poem from *Memos*, first published in the *Denver Quarterly*, was selected for *Best American Poetry 2015*. She's editor of *Spillway Magazine* and a poetry editor for *Pedestal Magazine*. http://www.susanterris.com

By Susan Terris

Poetry Books

Ghost of Yesterday: New & Selected Poems, 2013

The Homelessness of Self, 2011

Contrariwise, 2009

Natural Defenses, 2004

Fire Is Favorable to the Dreamer, 2003

Curved Space, 1998

Chapbooks

Dreamcrashers, 2016

Memos, 2015

All Generalizations Are Generalizations, 2014

Bar None, 2010

Chapbook on the Marketing of the Chapbook, 2009

Double-Edged, 2009

Sonya, The Doll-Wife, 2009

Wonder Bread Years, 2008

Marriage License, 2007

Block Party, 2007

Poetic License, 2004

Susan Terris: Greatest Hits, 2000

Minnesota Fishing Report, 2000

Eye of the Holocaust, 1999

Angels of Bataan, 1999

Killing in the Comfort Zone, 1995

Artist Books

Buzzards of Time, 2008

Sonya, The Doll-Wife, 2007

Tale of the Doll & the Bootless Child, 2011

Play

Whatever Self: Virginia Woolf & Virginia Woolf, 2016

Take Two: Film Studies
by Susan Terris

Cover photo by Bart Everson, from the Coca Cola filmstrip "Black Treasures" (1969)

Cover and interior set in Kabel LT STD and Joanna MT Std

Cover and interior design by Gillian Olivia Blythe Hamel

Offset printed in the United States
by Edwards Brothers Malloy, Ann Arbor, Michigan
On 55# Glatfelter B18 Antique
Acid Free Archival Quality Recycled Paper

Publication of this book was made possible in part by gifts from:
The Clorox Company
The New Place Fund
Robin & Curt Caton

Omnidawn Publishing
Oakland, California
2017
Rusty Morrison & Ken Keegan, senior editors & co-publishers
Gillian Olivia Blythe Hamel, managing editor
Cassandra Smith, poetry editor & book designer
Sharon Zetter, poetry editor, book designer & development officer
Avren Keating, poetry editor, fiction editor & marketing assistant
Liza Flum, poetry editor
Juliana Paslay, fiction editor
Gail Aronson, fiction editor
Trisha Peck, marketing assistant
Cameron Stuart, marketing assistant
Natalia Cinco, marketing assistant
Maria Kosiyanenko, marketing assistant
Emma Thomason, administrative assistant
SD Sumner, copyeditor
Kevin Peters, *OmniVerse* Lit Scene editor
Sara Burant, *OmniVerse* reviews editor